AN EAS'
SKETCHBOOK

60+ Years Visiting Virginia's Paradise

By

David Thatcher Wilson

Smith Beach Press

Thanks

This poor manuscript has been clunking around for sixteen years, now, in a semi-finished state. I play with it once in a while, and intend always to clean it up, expand upon it, and publish it online, but like so many projects, it languished. Today I got the incentive to finish it. Faye Wilson, a feisty nonagenarian from Eastville, said that it is time to update it and re-issue it. Well, she is right. So here we go. Thank you, Miss Faye.

I want to thank Poppa Jim and Molly and Little Jim and Al for introducing us to The Beach and The Bay. If it had not been for them I never would have discovered this little slice of paradise. Thanks Charlie for the wonderful down-home stories and introductions to some real characters. And to the people of Northampton County for being honest, loving, warm and wonderful

Some of the material in this book may seem dated. That is because it was first written as just a playful essay in 2000. There are some things that I will update, and others that I will not. If you are familiar with The Eastern Shore, you will understand why. Some stories might be apocryphal, being based on hearsay and memory. But I am not writing an academic tome. I am writing what I, and some others, fondly *think* we remember.

David Thatcher Wilson
Ft. Lauderdale, Florida

August 23, 2016

Prelude

Just as to New Yorkers there is only one city, The City, to me there is only one bay -- the Chesapeake, *The Bay*, the world's largest estuary. And on The Bay, on Virginia's lower Eastern Shore, is a one-mile long strip of sand called Smith Beach -- *The Beach*. That is what I am going to write about. *The Beach.* It's not just a place. The Beach is also a state of mind. An experience. A lifestyle. Almost a mystical way of being.

But the mysticism is not eternal. Sadly, it is threatened with more certain an extinction that the spotted owl or the snail darter, but for much the same reasons. "Progress" seems destined to destroy the experience of The Eastern Shore and The Beach. Incrementally, but inexorably. And, so, my paean to them both.

Fifty years ago, Virginia's Eastern Shore was fairly isolated. One highway traveled down from the north, US Route 13, and a single railroad track running beside it, but the only access from the south was via ferry from Little Creek, on the western bank of the Chesapeake, to Kiptopeake, over on The Shore. As a result, the way of life on The Shore was in stasis. Oh, there were changes. There had to be. But by and large, things remained small town. Farming community. American roots. Simple life. Norman Rockwell would have felt right at home.

In 1964 the ferry was replaced by The Chesapeake Bay Bridge-Tunnel, an 18-mile causeway that stretches from shore-to-shore, with two one - mile long tunnels to provide passage for large ships, and one high bridge. It was now possible to drive from the western shore to The Eastern Shore in under one-half hour! This opened the precious Shore up for discovery by more people. Luckily the original toll on the Bridge-Tunnel was sufficiently high to discourage day-trippers from discovering what was on the other side of The Bay. The fact that the Bridge-Tunnel Commission did not give commuting discounts certainly helped keep the traffic down on The Shore, although now there is a discount for over-and-back on the same day.

But progress is inexorable. A developer has bought up most of the property surrounding Cape Charles and is building up-scale housing developments with two golf courses, one designed by Nicklaus and the other by Palmer. This might be the definitive death knell for the overall way of life on The Shore. It remains to be seen.

It is because time marches on and "this, too, shall pass" that I felt it necessary to record my feelings and memories of The Shore and The Beach. It is truly a labor of love and adoration. I sincerely hope that it is not a eulogy.

Smith Beach

While walking together in the shallows of The Bay with my daughter, a few years ago, she said that her boss had asked if there was anything exciting to do at our beach house. Exciting? It's hard for people who haven't been there to understand *The Smith Beach Experience*. Today so many of us are adrenaline junkies, in constant need of bigger thrills, more excitement, greater stimulation. To many, vacation now means searching for our annual fix.

The whole Eastern Shore experience certainly is not that. Bucolic. That's what it is. With all that word encompasses -- countrified, agrarian, rustic, provincial, homey. When you live in south Florida (or New Jersey, or Philadelphia, or Richmond) it's just not what you're ready for . . . not what you'd expect. The Beach experience is . . . different. Wonderful, yes, but exciting it is not.

Eastville

The nearest town to the Beach is Eastville, the seat of Northampton County. It's a beautiful little town. The red brick county courthouse sits back from the road, with some old field pieces and memorials out in front and contains the oldest continuous records of any courthouse in the United States. I know, because one of the things to do on vacation at the Beach is to go up and visit the courthouse. No, there's no guided tour. Just check in with the County Clerk. If you ask nicely she'll show you some of the documents. The first one registered is a land transfer where a local Indian drew an eagle as his signature. There's an old paper from an early settler directing how he wished to be buried - in a coffin with a hinged end, which shall be interred upright, the hinged (door) above the ground. I guess he was afraid of being buried alive and wanted an escape hatch prepared.

There's also a Debtor's Prison. The Clerk has the key to that, too, and will let you borrow it to go check it out. Just up the road from the Courthouse sits the new post office. Well, it's actually about 30

years old, but here, that's new. It is right across the street from the tiny little brick building that used to be the post office. It's a surveyor's office, now.

The shopping area of Eastville? Well, right south of the Courthouse is the historic Eastville Inn. Two stories tall, white clapboard. It is registered as an historic building. But it's been closed for ages. I remember when I was a kid, back in the 50s, going in through the spring-slamming wooden screen door, and buying Slim Jims and Coke at the counter. Then it closed for a long time, until a young chef opened a very nice restaurant there. It was my absolute favorite restaurant in the world, with fresh crab and sweet potato biscuits. He had an herb garden out back where he grew his own herbs for cooking. That only lasted a few years, too, and now the hotel is vacant again. Looks pretty, though.

Across from the Hotel there is a store that used to be a drugstore. I can remember going in and shopping for comic books. Then, I think, it was a hardware store. After that an antique store. Big glass windows and a top floor that over hung the bottom. It's closed, now. Empty.

Eastville Hardware is just south of town on Business Route 13. You can buy hardware, fishing licenses and bait and gear, some car repair, and gardening implements. Right across the street was Gray's Furniture, but it's closed now. The volunteer fire department uses the building for bingo.

The little building just north of the hardware used to be Kate's Kupboard, a delightful bakery with fresh sticky buns each morning. I used to get up early, get the coffee perking, and drive up to the Kupboard for warm fresh cinnamon-y sticky buns. Kate moved on up the road to Exmore several years ago. In Eastville Kate's Kupboard is closed now. Nothing replaced it.

Next to that is a little place that started out as a soft ice cream stand. That lasted about a year. Someone used it as a residence for a while. Then it was a little church. Last I looked it was back to being a home. Things tend to get recycled here. Down the highway a piece stands a building with a cross on it, obviously built as a church that has been a home for as long as I can remember. But more on the recycling of buildings later.

Then, on the southwest corner, there's what is euphemistically called the Eastville Supermarket. We still think of it as B&B, from when Jack B. and his wife ran it. It's a dingy little everything-store with a laundromat next door, and a series of county-owned dumpsters in the side parking lot. I remember when Jack put the laundromat in. There's no sewer system, so he just ran the discharge pipes out back into the woods.

That is Eastville's business section. Pretty much all of it.

Just north of downtown is the high school. Way back, it was the "white" high school, when "separate but equal" was the rule, but since the 60s, of course, it is the Northampton County High School. There are some tennis courts out back of the school, but if you want to use them during the summer you had better take a push broom with you. They are usually thick with pine needles.

Just north of the high school is the Bethel A.M.E. Church. I don't know if the record still stands, but the church used to be listed in the Guinness Book of World Records as having more corners than any other church.

Cape Charles

The biggest nearby "city" is Cape Charles, and Cape Charles does have a business area. Downtown, the central business district, is just about two blocks long. How wide? Well, two blocks long. Used to have a Peebles Department Store, the place mom and Molly Dixon would go shop for everything from shorts to bathing suits to reading glasses. And there was a movie theater, too. We never went there, for some reason. I guess that just was not one of the things one did on vacation at the Beach. The State ABC Store used to be there for a long time, but they moved up on the highway. Makes more sense to sell booze in a high traffic area.

There is a homosexual gentrification going on in Cape Charles, so there are some little art shops, specialty bakeries and cutesy shoppes opening, along with pubs and coffee shops and a few restaurants. They are buying up and refurbishing many of the beautiful old homes, although a pastel-colored home in Cape Charles does look somewhat out of place. The down-home farmers are rather bemused by the whole thing.

The ferry from Norfolk used to dock here, and this still is the southern terminus of the railroad, where the boxcars can be loaded onto barges and ferried across the Bay. Indeed, fishing from the dock used to be problematic, with the chance of snagging on one of the numerous boxcars that had rolled off into the water. But that ended years ago.

At the eastern end of Mason Street, the main downtown street, the end away from the beach, there used to be an ice house where you could buy ice and dry ice - ice for keeping the fish fresh when you were out fishing, and dry ice to keep things cold all the long drive back to New Jersey. It was pretty dilapidated even in the 1950s, but functioning. The ice house is gone, now, replaced by drug store. A big chunk of rusted machinery sits there in the grass. Kind of looks like ancient industrial art.

Cape Charles even had a country club. The Northampton Country Club. Well, it called itself a country club. Actually, it was more like a cow pasture golf course. Nine holes with two sets of tees at each hole so you could play 18 "different" holes. There were water hazards and sand traps, and seagulls that strut around the fairways and greens just daring you to hit a ball close to them. But it was real down home friendly, even if you did occasionally have to turn off the sprinklers yourself to putt out. I remember playing there when the greens fee was $5 for all day. Not for a round. All day. Play a round, go home for lunch and a nap, go on back and do it again.

Cape Charles has a number of beautiful, huge, old red brick homes that face out to The Bay over the public beach, and several square blocks of restored and not-so-nice homes throughout. There is a little library, in an old building that used to be a church (remember the building recycling?), and the town water tower is painted to look just like a lighthouse. It's cute.

Drive-In Movie

The exciting things to do on vacation at The Beach? Well, there used to be a drive-in movie up the road a piece, but it closed years ago.

Cheriton

Cheriton is the little town between Eastville and Cape Charles. In town Paul's used to be the combination drugstore/restaurant/soda fountain/bus stop. It was one of the focal points for us. After church we'd stop by for an ice cream and to look at comic books. Paul was usually sitting in a big old leather easy chair behind the counter where he sold the bus tickets and miscellany. We'd sit at the fountain eating ice cream and visiting, or reading a comic book, watching the occasional car go by. Back then there was not a lot of traffic on Route 13.

All-of-a-sudden a string of twenty cars would go by headed north up Route 13. A veritable traffic jam! Then you'd know that the ferry had docked at Kiptopeake and discharged its cargo. That was excitement!

The seafood at Paul's was great, having come fresh from either the Bay or the nearby ocean. And the pies! Paul's cooks made the finest sweet potato pie in the world. Mom would always ask for the recipe, but whenever she did, they told her that the baker just happened to be out at that time. No matter what time it was. Special recipes are something to be guarded on The Shore. She never did get that recipe.

Right next door to Paul's was Rolley's (pronounced Raw'-leys). That was the general store. Some few groceries, seeds, tools, dust, flypaper, fishin' stuff, tin chimney fittings, and such. Old Mr. Rolley would usually be there, sitting around with a bunch of friends jawin'. Son Francis pretty much ran the store, leaving Mr. Rolley time to visit. Mr. Rolley lived in the big square yaller house just out of town on Route 13, pretty much across from the migrant camp. Rolley's is closed, now. And the migrant camp is gone like it never existed.

"Hop" used to have a Chevy dealership in town, but that closed years ago. When Route 13 bypassed the town with its new four-lane highway, Cheriton got really quiet.

Hop kept a nice Owens cabin cruiser out at King's Creek Marina. The Wild Rose. He told me that it was named after an old rum runner's boat. Since he owned the Chevy dealership Hop used to regularly drop new engines into The Wild Rose. He used to brag to me that when both engines were running wide open, each would take a stream of gasoline "as big as your little finger". Of course, gasoline was a lot cheaper then. He could open both engines up, and three-quarters of that 28' cabin cruiser would come out of the water on a plane. Powerful. I went out fishing with Hop one time, on the Wild Rose. We were drifting in the channel, not having a lot of luck, when all of a sudden we drifted backward up onto a sandbar and stuck. Hop walked to the back of the boat, looked over the transom, went to the controls and threw both engines in full forward. Kind of dug a new channel out of the bar. Got us free, though. That was Hop. I guess he's gone, now, him and his wife Sassy.

On Sunday we'd go up to the Cheriton Methodist Church. I don't remember much about church, except that everyone sat in the back pews and everyone was hot. It was the first time I ever saw fans in church. Not electric fans. In the rack on the back of each pew, there with the hymnal and the King James Bible, were cardboard fans with flat wooden handles that looked kind of like tongue depressors stapled on. On one side of the fan would be a lithograph of some colorful scene from the Bible, and on the other would be some words. Now that I think of it, they were probably Bible verses, but I never read them. Fans in church. It would be fun, watching the motion of all those fans. Some ladies would be real slow and gentle with their motion, and some of the younger ones would try to get a real hurricane of wind flapping. You could pretty much tell who was asleep, too. They'd just be sitting sweating, not fanning. Then, after church, we'd head to dinner at Paul's, and back to The Beach. Unless we stopped by to visit Chris and Clarence or Ralph and Irma or Wilsie or Kitty. Visiting was as much a part of the Smith Beach Experience as anything. They're pretty much all gone, now.

Big Jim was raised in Cheriton, in a section called Sunnyside. I remember a story he told about his parents, Alvin and Mamie. I knew Mamie, Grandma Dick as we called her. She lived with Poppa Jim and the family at home in New Jersey. Seems a stray cat showed up at their house in Sunnyside. The thing looked hungry, so they fed it [big mistake], and then Grandpa Alvin took the cat to work with him, down at the Cheriton train station. Next morning, there was the cat back for breakfast. This time Grandpa Alvin took the cat, rode several stops north, and left it at another depot telling the manager there what was up. The manager, who apparently had a good sense of humor, drove home to Cheriton that night with the cat in the car, and let it out near Grandpa Alvin's. Next morning, there's the cat waiting for breakfast! This time Grandpa gives the cat to a trainman headed north and tells him to keep the cat until he gets to Maryland. Well, he did. And in Maryland he gave the cat to a trainman headed south and told him to turn it loose in Cheriton. When they found the cat on the doorstep again the next morning Grandma Mamie allowed that they might as well keep it 'cause they sure couldn't get rid of it.

A block south of Paul's you turn east between the Baptist and Methodist churches. A few blocks up, just past the tracks, you can still see the old brick smokestack for Webster's cannery. I can remember as a kid looking at ketchup labels in restaurants, and being excited when I'd find Webster's, Cheriton, VA. The tomato fields are still producing, but Webster's closed years ago.

Keep driving down this road, though, and we will reach Oyster.

Oyster

Continue on this road for just a few miles to Oyster. It's a shame - Oyster is still quaint, but it is falling apart more and more. It isn't development that is killing Oyster, but neglect.

There is a nice little well-protected fishing harbor, but there aren't many active fishing boats left. Used to be that the ocean-going clam dredgers tied up there, but not anymore. With its old wooden boats, some beached hulks, its tiny one-room post office,

and its little Chapel by the Sea, Oyster is still picturesque.

There used to be a bunch of fish packing sheds along the harbor, where you could buy menhaden for bait or fresh fish for eating. And there were mountains of the shells of the bivalves that gave Oyster its name.

And at the very end of the town was a weathered, deserted, two-story hotel that overlooked the salt water flats toward the ocean. I don't know if it was storms or vandals or "urban renewal," but the hotel has been gone for years.

Not far from the old hotel lay a high grassy sandbar called Horse Island. Fifty years ago, we used to wait until low tide and wade out through the black mud and muck and myriads of fiddler crabs to Horse Island to look for flint Indian arrowheads. The island had an old Indian burial ground on it, and if we walked long enough with our eyes to the ground we could find shaped flints and arrowheads, some quite beautiful black flint.

Across the harbor from the town is a State-maintained boat ramp. It's a convenient place to put in if you are going to fish over on seaside. I remember, back before the state improved it, Blind Bill used to have a shack there where he sorted clams, sizing them by feel. We would stop and visit a bit and buy some bait clams from him before launching our little Chincoteague scow to go out fishing.

It's a long way out to the ocean, weaving through the grass and marsh flats. A little more than half way out, off to your left, are the weather-beaten pilings and brick chimneys of what once was a substantial hotel. This used to be a popular area for wealthy folks from "up north" to come hunting and fishing. The hotel closed and burned over 60 years ago.

Further out is Cobb Island. This is where the old Coast Guard Station stood. Three stories, with a lookout cupola on the top, wooden clapboard which once was painted white. There's still an empty boathouse, with its doors ajar and rusty rails running down to the little protected lagoon. The windows have all been broken out, either from the vandalism of man or the vandalism of the ever-present weather. Cobb Island Coast Guard Station is just north of Wreck Island. I wonder if that means anything. The Cobb Island Coast Guard Station was closed and abandoned years ago. Just recently they put the old station on a barge and moved it to Oyster. Why? Good question. It is nice that they did not just abandon it to the elements.

If you remember your bug spray walking on the beach on Cobb or Wreck Islands can be very enjoyable. I used to have my parents put me ashore on Wreck to explore while they fished the inlet. Absolutely deserted. Lots of shells. Lots of flotsam. Occasional pieces of Navy ordnance or sonobouys. Interesting. Just don't pick up the wrong thing and blow your hand off. Mom would get mad.

The Deep Road

Route 13, the Lankford Highway, is the main artery of The Shore, running right down the center. It's a divided four-lane road, now, and there are still a number of accidents each year by local folks who have trouble coping with the speed of a Yankee-driven car racing south.

Used to be Route 13 was only three lanes ... one lane north, one lane south, and a suicide lane in the middle for whoever had the courage (or had achieved the frustration level) to pull out and pass. It was real exciting to pull out to pass a tractor-pulled farm wagon and find someone coming the other way who had the same idea at the same time. At night I remember you would flip your high-beams on when you pulled out to pass. Whether this was to illuminate the road, warn other drivers, or try to intimidate anyone coming the other direction who wanted to pass also, I'm not sure. Of course, if two of you were headed in opposite directions were out there blinding each other with your hi-beams, things could get a little dicey.

Before the four-lane Route 13 ran right through the center of all the towns - Birdsnest, Exmore, Painter, Onley and Bloxom. Most of them got bypassed with the new four-lane, like Cheriton. Some have recovered. Some have not.

To get to The Beach you turn west off old (business) Route 13 just south of Eastville, right next to B&B. This road, down from 13, used to be called "The Deep Road," because of the high hardwood trees growing close on either side of the road for the first mile or so. Just a short way down The Deep Road from B&B there used to be two white lines painted vertically across the road. We didn't tell our parents, but they were painted just ¼ mile apart, The Deep Road Dragstrip.

After the "deep" part of the road the land opens up to fields. This first one, on the right, is usually planted with tomatoes. It's the only field I've seen that is irrigated from below! You can see the pipes and pumps at the well on the corner, from where the pipes stretch all under the field. This was a radical idea when installed.

One thing that I find fascinating about old farmlands are the occasional deserted houses you see standing out in a field. There were a couple of these down The Deep Road. I like to reflect on the men that built them, and on the families that lived in them, the children who were born and grew up in them. I wonder when they fell vacant, and why, and I wonder whether any of the former residents ever pass by and have memories of how it used to be.

There used to be two deserted houses on the road down to The Beach. Gray never-painted weathered boards, patchy shingle roofs, tumbledown porches. Each year there would look to be some migrant workers camping out in them, but each year they would seem to disintegrate more and more, until finally they were gone. As kids, we always kind of wondered if they were haunted. Never had the courage to go see.

As you drive down the road did you notice that everyone who passes seems to wave? Do you know them? No, that's just the way it is out here. Everyone is friendly. Everyone waves. You are in a different world, at The Beach. You are on The Eastern Shore.

Keep going until the road sort of forks, and the main road bends to the left. You want to go to the right, but if you had taken the left road you would go by the field where the hotel used to be. There was a three-story green-and-white wooden hotel right there on Wilkins Beach. It closed years ago. In fact, it disappeared completely over thirty years ago. But it used to be a landmark. There is now a VORTAC on the site.

That's an airplane directional beacon for the Norfolk Airport, across the Bay. We don't need one over here. The closest airport, for general aviation, is over an hour up the road. Most people who fly on The Shore just use a local field. Not airfield. Field. But more about that later.

There's a line of trees just south of the VORTAC, running from the street to the beach. If you turn there you can drive all the way to the Bay. Park there, climb down the bank to the beach, turn south and you can walk for over a mile without seeing people nor houses. You've got to pick your way over piles of bleached driftwood, but the photo opportunities are magnificent. Bay on the right, pinewoods and sand dunes on the left. Climb up over the lower dunes and you find a little brackish pond with ducks in it. Beautiful.

But we took the right fork. The Beach road. Follow it down about one-half mile and it takes a 90-degree bend to the right. Before you turn, though, you can see the Bay through a gap in the trees right in front of you. If you are coming down from the north for vacation, this is the first glimpse of the Bay you'll get. Turn the corner and you are at The Beach.

The Beach

The Beach is a mile-long strip of "civilization" on the Bay. It has cottages all the way down on the Bay side, and now most of the way on the land side of the road, too. The cottages are mostly summer places. Used to be that it was local farmers who owned them. They'd occasionally rent them to vacationers. There were only a very few that were occupied year-round. Come to think of it, there still are only a few that see winter use. But now there are owners from a lot of different places. I wonder how they all ever heard of The Beach.

The homeowners are just that - home-owners. The property of Smith Beach is still owned by the family of Tom Smith. Tom is gone, now. I can remember him, forty-five years ago, driving his white pickup truck up and down the road.

Tom was a bachelor, and he had a big farmhouse down a lane that runs back from Smith Beach Road. I think the lane's named "Tom's Road." Original. He and his brother used to live together in the big house. They say that one day Tom and his brother had a big argument and in anger his brother went out, climbed into his little airplane parked in a back field, and took off. Tom, still being angry, hooked the disc harrow up to his tractor and plowed the field so that his brother couldn't land there again. Least that's what they tell. And that's the way it is at The Beach.

The cottages, up and down the road, are an interesting amalgam. "The Preacher's Cottage," which our friends used to rent, had two bedrooms (to get to the back bedroom you had to walk through the front bedroom) and a tin roof. I believe that it started life as a packing shed, then got hauled to the beach to become a cottage. There's a tiny bathroom that for years didn't have a window. Finally, Clarence, the ancient local plumber who looked after the cottage for the preacher, cut a hole to the bathroom in the outside wall. He made a screened wood-slat louvered "window," and it was done. We found, during a powerful rainstorm, that the wooden louvers just weren't sufficient, and I remember Dad and Big Jim trying to tack plastic over the window with the wind and the rain and the sand whistling through, and the plastic snapping like a flag in the breeze.

The flooring was old linoleum, laid over the plywood, and it wasn't nailed or glued down. We found that out when we were brushed by the winds of a hurricane. Our poor English Setter, Lassie, truly freaked out when the winds blew, and floor started rising and falling like a boat on the Bay.

And the pump! All the cottages are on wells, and in "The Preacher's Cottage" when the pump out back would come on the whole place would vibrate. You always knew when someone got up to use the bathroom in the middle of the night from the way the house would pulsate. It was fun.

The first cottage that we rented was down at the other end of the road. Near The Gulf. There was a hill, then a little curve back in the beach, and that's where we were. The way the cottage was situated, in the lee of the hill, we were protected from storms. We were also protected from any breezes, and this was in the years before air conditioning. It was sweltering all day and most of the night. These cottages were basically "weekenders," and it was before a lot of stuff became commonplace. Like hot water heaters. In this cottage we did have solar hot water. That meant that there was a hot water tank on the roof, and the sun was supposed to heat the water. It probably would have worked fine, except that the tank was painted white, like the cottage. It reflected the sun's heat rather than absorbed it, the way a black tank would. Cold showers for two weeks. Well, at least we did have indoor plumbing.

Many, maybe most, of the cottages at The Beach were buildings that had been brought in from somewhere else. Charlie Matthews owned five that were war-surplus, and that he had brought across the Bay after the war. He named all his cottages after species of duck. Pintail, widgeon, mallard.

One cottage used to be the train depot in Weirwood, just up Route 13. It was being abandoned, so some enterprising person popped it onto a flatbed and trucked it down to The Beach. They fixed it up real nice. Still has the WEIRWOOD station sign on the side.

On the field-side of the road there are a couple of long cottages ... long with long front screened-in porches. They used to be vegetable packing sheds ... sliding doors and all. Trucked them down to The Beach, knocked together some interior walls, and

PRESTO! Summer cottages.

Did you notice the big white cottage about six up from the corner on the Bayside? That one used to be the second-floor apartment over a country store, years ago. The owner was going to tear the whole building down, so they knocked out everything below, dropped the top floor down onto a flatbed, and hauled it on down to The Beach.

Then there's the place where Hefty used to live. It's on the field side. Good old Hefty. He used to come up from Florida and spend a few weeks or the entire summer. Then one year, he came up and stayed. Hefty put a trailer across from Bob and Retha's little summer trailer, and he and Lucille and daughter Martha moved in. Named it "Starve Easy." Over the years Hefty added on an all-weather front porch/living room in the front, and a big master bedroom in the back. He used to joke that he was ready for anything - the porch was heated by electric baseboards, the main trailer had an oil heater, and the big master bedroom had gas heat. It was nice. He added a nice little screened-in porch as a vestibule, and a laundry room at the other end. Hefty was talking with a visitor to his home and mentioned his trailer. "You've got a trailer, too?" the visitor asked.

Hefty had added on so much all around the core trailer that you no longer see much of it there.

Across the street from Hefty, and a couple of houses up, some folks wanted to put a big side porch on their home, but they didn't want to cut down the tall shade tree that was there. So, they built around it, and have the tree growing right up through the porch roof.

Our cottage used to be the old print shop up in Eastville. Someone picked it up and hauled it down to The Beach, then started adding on. A weatherized front porch, two bedrooms on the side, then a master bedroom in the back, and a pump house ... it just kind of grew to where it is now. Rachel suggested that we follow a tradition at The Beach and give our cottage a name. She wants to call it Paradise Found. When she said that it got me thinking about the other cottages, up and down the road, and the names their owners have given them.

I'm sure there were others, but the first home I remember being named was Hefty's. When he retired to The Beach from Florida he named his cottage Starve Easy. I always liked that. Since the cottage passed down to Smith and Martha they've kept the name. Of course. Tradition and heritage mean a lot on The Eastern Shore.

As you drive in the first house on the road has a sign that says POSTED NO TRESPASSING KEEP OUT. If that's what they named their cottage, I'm not impressed.

Remember the big white house when we started up the road?

Reggie and Pam have named it The Crooked White House. I think it was done tongue-in-cheek. You recall that the cottage used to be the top floor of a store. Just like our cottage, The Crooked White House has a lot of add-ons, making it ... well, crooked. Actually, it's kind of interesting. At the north end of their lot they've tied four little wooden barn-sheds together to make one long storage area.

Next door Colonel Adams has named his place At Ease. As retired military, myself, I like that. It's a lot cuter than when Ches and Nora Wise called it Wise Cottage. Very nice people, Ches and Nora. Not a lot of imagination in naming their cottage.

The other side of Reggie and Pam is Twasadump.

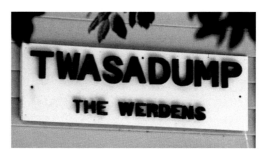

T'was one, too. I visited it years ago when Tommy Wilson and his family rented there. Certainly is an attractive place, now.

Next door to Hefty's is the old Weirwood train station. Yep, put it on a flatbed and brought it down. It's so spiffed up that the only way you know it used to be a train station is from the red-and-yellow WEIRWOOD depot sign still up on the south side of the home.

Yankee Land is the two-story owned by Jan and Eileen. They are from Connecticut and aren't ashamed to admit that they are "come here's," as opposed to "from here's." Eventually they'll be "stay here's." [What's the old joke? "What's the difference between a 'Yankee' and a 'damn Yankee'? A Yankee goes home again."] Yankee Land used to be a shacky little one-story place when Tommy Fox still owned it as a rental. Jan and Eileen have torn down and added on so much, I wonder if any of the original structure's still there.

Tommy Fox, the daddy, used to be the undertaker. (I believe that 'young' Tommy still is.) Dad used to joke that he often got worried when he'd shake hands with Tommy and Tommy'd ask, "How're you feeling?" Dad was always afraid that Tommy was out drumming up business.

On up the road there's Stumpy's Hideaway.

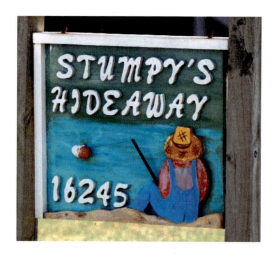

Ol' Stumpy was dying of cancer but he still used to ride his little golf cart up and down the road to visit neighbors. That is until the game warden told him that it was illegal to drive it on a public road and made him stop. Poor Stumpy. He's gone, now.

There's a new sign out at one cottage - Four Sea Sons. I don't know the folks, but it is honoring their four boys. Cute. Of course, I hear she's pregnant, again. I wonder if they'll change the name of their place.

Uncle Carl Weisiger named their place 3 C's.

I used to know who the 3 "C's" were. There was Uncle Carl. His eldest son Carl Owen ... but then there were David, Brent, and Aunt Ernie.

I don't know. Brent's still around. I'll have to ask him some day.

Next door to Chris Wilson, the contractor, is Conched Out.

I like that. Others, up and down the road, are Pelican Point, Out to Pasture, there are two Roost's, the Russells and Roberts, Donovan's Reef [a great John Wayne/Lee Marvin movie], The Last Resort, Honker Flats, Saturday Cottage, Paradise on The Bay, and Hullabaloo and Chaos Too. I'd love to know the story behind that one.

Our next-door neighbor is

Others up and down the road are:

Another house, down at The Beach, used to be the train depot up in Nassawadox. It was abandoned by the railroad, and the Town decided to sell the building to get rid of an eyesore. It was bought by a Smith Beach resident who intended to haul it down for a beach cottage. That was until some of the Nassawadox "heritage and history" people got involved. "How could the Town sell such a valuable [?] piece of its history?" They were all up in arms, and it looked like the sale was going to be reversed. So, the Smith Beach-er waited until one dark night, went on up with a truck, hooked up the depot, and started hauling it back to The Beach. When the County Sheriff stopped him out on Route 13, he explained that he was just hauling this old building he had bought down to Smith Beach to set up as a cottage, and he got a police escort the whole way! It wasn't until the next morning that the folks in Nassawadox realized that the sale had been consummated, and their historic train depot was now a cottage at Smith Beach. But that's the way it is on The Eastern Shore, and part of the Smith Beach Experience.

One summer when we arrived there was a railroad caboose sitting on the side of the road at the top of the hill near The Gulf. Someone had brought it down and set it up as a guesthouse! It was not painted the red of a regular caboose, though. It was named The Chartreuse Caboose, and that was its color. I always wanted to see inside it, but I never got the chance. It was there for a couple of years, and then, one year, it was gone again. Like I said, the homes down here are picked up and moved in from all sorts of places.

The Gulf

At the north end of The Beach the road ends at The Gulf. That's a saltwater creek [or crick] that runs from the Bay all the way in close up to Eastville. It isn't navigable all that way, and for the part that is, mostly that's just at high tide. We used to water-ski back in The Gulf when I was a kid. It was real flat, and we had a shallow draft boat which we would keep up on a plane so we wouldn't hit bottom. You didn't want to fall, though. Seemed like all the stinging nettle jellyfish in the world liked the warm water back up The Gulf, and the shallow bottom was covered with oyster shells which could cut you up pretty good.

We used to crab in The Gulf. Out in The Bay, too. Big blue crabs. Delicious. We didn't need chicken neckin' or pots. Just put a bushel basket in an innertube and tie it so it floats behind you as you walk in the shallows with a crab net and dip them up. Used to be, when the grasses still grew in The Bay and The Gulf, you could dip up maybe a half-bushel of Jimmies. We'd always throw the Sukes back so they could have more babies. Can't dip crabs anymore. Personally, I think it's the water quality and the death of the grass beds, but they just aren't there anymore. We put out two pots in the channel, out front of the house, but some summers it's just a waste of good chicken backs.

Joe Downes, Sr. wrote and reminded me of some things. Actually (forgive me, Joe) he remembers stuff from before I even heard of Smith Beach! Man!

Almost everybody at The Beach has a boat. If you've read anything I've written before this you know that if you don't like the water, then there's nothing for you to do at The Beach. Joe reminded me of Tom Smith's boat. Down at The Gulf, right next to the ramp where we could launch our boats, was a locked boathouse. If you peeked in through a crack in the door, or hunkered down and looked in through the end, you could see Tom Smith's boat hanging there. If I remember correctly it was a gorgeous, shiny-varnished Chris Craft. Is that right, Joe? I don't ever remember seeing it in the water, but Joe remembers riding in Tom's boat. He tells me that back before there was a road to the boathouse, if you would help Tom carry five-gallon cans of gasoline through the woods to the boat, he'd take you water skiing. One year when we arrived the boathouse, and the boat, were gone.

The Beach, again

Chris and Rachel were scandalized, the other day. Mid-summer and there were 32 other people on the beach within eyesight (that's at least a mile)!

And on the weekends there are sometimes two jet skis! Last night, for the first time in memory, a car drove by with its radio turned high enough to be able to "feel" the bass inside the house. That's not the Smith Beach Experience.

Today is Monday, a beautiful sunny day, and there are NO people on the beach! The call of the gulls, the whistling of the breeze,

and an occasional car driving by. THAT is the Smith Beach Experience. The predominant sound is the song of mockingbirds. Or the angry cry of the mockingbird in its attack mode as she dive-bombs the poor dog. And, too, there is the call of the bobwhite quail as she whistles to keep her kids together. This morning, as Chris and Rachel drove up the road to buy a newspaper, mom and a covey of little babies ran across the road in front of them, headed from one field to another. That is the Smith Beach Experience.

Another part of it is the fact that the phone man just came to fix the telephone. He was due yesterday. We stuck around from 0800 to 1900 hours, and he came at 1130 today. That is definitely the Smith Beach Experience. Actually, that's pretty prompt.

The work ethic on The Eastern Shore is interesting. Chris Wilson builds a lot of the beach steps, decks and seawalls. He does a very good job.

But he's got a cell phone, and if he gets the call that the fish are running, he's gone. Chris makes no bones about it. He has his priorities!

Chris was building a fancy set of decks and stairs next door when he got the call. Finally, about dark, I went over, picked up his power tools out of the yard, and moved them to the porch. Not that they'd get stolen. Didn't want the heavy dew to get them. I think it was a couple of days before he got back.

But Chris does really nice work. When he built our stairs, knowing that I'm crippled and my parents were old, he put each step an inch or two closer together. He always sands off the sharp edges of the boards, too. Not a major thing, maybe, but a nice quality touch. He finally gets it done, and when he does it's a work of art, not just construction. When it is finally done. It helps if you happen to be a fellow Freemason. You just have to understand the Smith Beach timetable and priorities.

The deck that Chris built us is a wonderful place

to sit and watch and generally contemplate life. I wrote this while doing so:

> As I sit on the deck overlooking the Chesapeake, I wonder -- the blossoms on the Virginia Creeper are so red and luscious, why aren't there any hummingbirds feeding from them? It could be the pretty stiff breeze blowing in from The Bay is too hard for them to hold station while they dip their beaks, but down the bank it is a bit more sheltered. Then I discovered one of the reasons as a tiny little hummingbird races past me being chased off by a big black-and-yellow bumblebee. Doesn't like the competition, I guess.

Other Sensory Experiences

Now, I don't want to seem ghoulish, but pain is part of The Smith Beach Experience, too. Who can forget walking barefoot across the front lawn only to find that the sand spurs have been flourishing this year? Little gray prickly pincushions created by Satan himself. And trying to pull those devilishly sharp things from your feet, you only end up with them stuck in your fingers. Or how about the sun? I remember well the time Jimmy and I walked way down the Beach, feeling the sun burning into our backs. Felt good. Until that night. Then the mothers spent the evening making strong tea, soaking rags in it, and gently laying them on our crisped backs so that the tannic acid would ease the pain. Oh, yes.

Definitely a painful part of The Smith Beach Experience. And who can forget mom trying to dig out a splinter from deep in the meaty part of your sole with a sewing needle? Yeah. Shoes weren't optional, they <u>were not worn</u>. So various foot pains became part of The Smith Beach Experience.

Stinging nettles, the jellyfish kind, were part of the experience, too. They were beautiful, translucent, gossamer ghosts floating just below the surface of the water. They'd have long lacy trailing skirts that billowed out behind them. Some would have tinges of red and blue in them. Gorgeous! Until you came into contact with those "lacy trailing skirts." Then they were pure pain. When you were looking the other way, maybe getting ready to try to get up on water-skis, or waiting to try to dunk Dad, the nettle would drift with the current up against you and wrap those tentacles around you. As kids we thought it was acid, as the burning would spread wherever we were touched. There were lots of remedies for nettle stings, though I don't remember any of them working particularly well. The first thing we would do would be to grab a handful of sand from the bottom and scrub away at the stinging area. In retrospect, that probably just made things worse. Mom would crank out her trustworthy bottle of ammonia. I think that now the preferred treatment is a paste of meat tenderizer. I don't know why! Ask someone's mom. That's just what they tell me! James Michener recommended urine, but what kid is going to let his friend pee on him? When we would ski back up The Gulf the water would be wall-to-wall nettles. I guess they liked the warm water. Always gave us a great incentive not to fall.

I'm pretty sure I mentioned the bugs before. But until yesterday I had forgotten what happens when the wind shifts. When the wind shifts so that it is no longer coming in off the water, but is now an "offshore breeze," it brings all the biting black flies from the farmlands. That's when you stay either under the water or in the house. You've got to remember to brush all the flies off the dog's back when you let her in, or the house will fill up quickly. No, it isn't as bad as all that, and the wind has shifted back to onshore, so the flies have gone. Don't worry.

I first learned about redbugs, chiggers, at Smith Beach. Mom found some blackberry brambles back off the road down near The Gulf. Dad loved blackberry mush on his ice cream, so we went off blackberry picking. It wasn't long after that we found these welts on our legs. Itch? I want to tell you!!!! Mom tried all her old remedies – a poultice of baking soda, a paste of meat tenderizer, swab on ammonia [you think that wasn't stimulating after you'd already scratched the welt open?] – all to no avail. Once those buggers get under your skin they are harder to get rid of than a mother-in-law! We never did figure it out, then. I guess I just scratched until they had lived their cycle and died. Now I know better. I send my kids to pick the berries, and I stay home in front of the fan with a good book. Being the daddy has its advantages.

Smells. That is another part of the Beach experience. No, not just the smell of frying fish or chicken [though I won't complain about them]. I remember when I first returned to The Shore after coming home from Viet Nam. Driving across the Bridge-Tunnel the tide was out, and when we reached The Shore I could smell the rich, kind of rotten, a little gamy smell of the black mud that the low tide exposed. I smelled some things in Viet Nam that were a lot worse, and I've smelled expensive perfume, but that smell of Chesapeake Bay black mud, smelling of decomposing shellfish and sea grass and salt water and who-knows-what is one of the nicest aromas around.

And at night . . . there's still the smell of honeysuckle. Oh, sure, I've smelled honeysuckle elsewhere. But it mixes in with all the other smells – The Bay, new cut grass, fish, new turned earth, crabs boiling, watermelon – to be part of the Beach experience.

Food

Food is another important part of The Smith Beach Experience. Yes, indeed. Fresh fish either dropped off by friends or caught yourself; fresh vegetables, either bought from roadside stands right on the edge of the fields or picked from the fields yourself. You can still come home from church on a Sunday to find a paper sack of tomatoes or sweet corn sitting by the door. Or Charlie might drop by with a basket of oysters he just tonged. Or Tim might drop by on his way back from fishing with a mess of croaker or weakfish. It's all in the family. The Smith Beach Experience.

This might be a good place to mention the fresh produce. Jim and Molly, having grown up locally, in Cheriton and Willis Wharf, knew many of the local farmers personally. They'd contact them when a field had been picked over, and we'd get permission to go in and pick what the pickers, the migrant workers, had left or missed. And that was a lot! Mostly I remember it was tomatoes and corn, and those, along with the fish, became absolute staples of Smith Beach cuisine. Although I could never do it, I remember Mom picking a tomato, and then eating it like an apple!

We usually dressed the part for these picking forays, too. Mom and Molly would wear big floppy hats; Molly's was often a straw fishing hat with a green plastic visor. We'd be dressed in ratty old tee-shirts, shorts, dirty sneakers. I am sure that we looked like white migrant workers ourselves. I am also sure that my sister, who would have been a teenager at the time, was just dying in embarrassment. Not that there was anyone around to notice us.

But talk about food! Watch in the local weekly newspaper (or, if you are high-tech, on Billy Barton's email newsletter) for church suppers. You want to talk about good eating!? Everyone is welcome, and the ladies of the church do the cooking. You just can't go to any restaurant, even those that proclaim "home cooking," and find the succulent quality of the sweet potato biscuits, soft-shell crabs, steamed clams, oyster and clam fritters, fried chicken, cantaloupe and watermelon that you will find at a church dinner. And all of it that you can eat, sitting at tables in the church's side yard. What an experience! Makes me hungry just writing about it.

I remember one such church dinner, I guess it was up near Exmore. I finished my meal and said to mom that I was going back for some more clam fritters. A man, whom I did not know, asked me to pick up a few for him, too. I did, of course, and Mr. Tankard, who it was, invited me to stop by his drugstore the next time I was in Exmore and he'd give me a free ice cream cone. That was when drugstores usually had soda fountains, too. I was always proud of my "relationship" with such an important man.

Food. It seems that little restaurants were always popping up and closing on The Shore. I remember Charlie took us to one, once. It was way back off Route 13. The advertised (at least by word-of-mouth) draw for that spot was that the proprietor would take out his teeth, pull his lower lip up over his top one, and talk funny. Well, I guess you had to be there to appreciate it. Or not, come to think of it.

The Shower

If you have ever been to the beach in the summer, you know what it is like to come up from the beach and you are hot and sandy and salty and tired? That is all part of summer vacation, right? Well, instead of tracking all that wet sand through the house, and getting mom angry with you,

get into the outdoor shower. It is enclosed so as not to scandalize the neighbors, but open on top so you can feel the sun warm on your body with the cool water running down. You can rinse out your bathing suit and leave it to drip before hanging it on the line, but don't forget to take a towel to wrap around you before ducking back inside the house.

Or go out at night for your bedtime shower and feel the warm water while you feel the cool night breezes and look up at the stars. Blissful! Of course, you do have to watch out that the mosquitoes or horse flies don't bite you. Especially when you are in the all-and-all in the shower. Scratching those bites in public could be embarrassing. And make certain that you rinse the sand off your feet in the bucket by the door before you go back in the house.

Mother Nature Wins

Remember the margarine commercial about "It's not nice to fool Mother Nature?" That really comes into play at The Beach. Each winter the storms seem to eat away more of the beach and the bank out front of the house. When I was much younger I remember Clarence telling me that he could recall when they farmed out as far as the second sandbar.

That's about two- to three-hundred feet, now. They've tried lots of ways to slow or stop the erosion. First, they put in rows of railroad ties, like pilings, to try to catch the sand. Started with them up against the bank stretching down into the water. The ones that are left, they're mostly all the way out in the water, now, with the bank eaten away behind them.

One year the Mahalykas tried putting railroad tie pilings across the front of the bank and dumping broken up road concrete down behind it. Ches Wise tried it, too. Mother Nature took it all. Uncle Carl dumped huge chunks of rock and concrete all over the bank in front of his cottage. Kind of worked.

Down by the Vortac the government put big sand-filled bags to stop the erosion. Nope. Winter storms undercut the bags, and they collapsed, flopping down into the surf.

Then they put loads of riprap, stones, on the bank in front of the Vortac. Well, it stopped the erosion directly in front, but the winter waves cut in on either side and made it into a peninsula. They finally had to pick up the Vortac and move it further back from the edge.

I remember one summer seeing a house, down past the Vortac that got fully undercut and collapsed down onto the beach.

At our house dad put off trying any bulkheads for years because he knew that if his bulkheads worked, the tides and storms would wash away the banks of our neighbors on either side. We finally went ahead and put up bulkheads and groynes to protect our bank. Sure enough, that winter the storms did not devastate our bank, but they did cut about eight feet of the neighbor's bank and wash it away. In the battle of man against nature ... bet on nature.

Sounds

It might not be exciting to city-folk, but I always enjoyed watching the birds at The Beach. When Dad would fillet the fish we caught (or when Jonathan does it now), he'd toss the carcasses down to the beach as he worked. When he began there might not be a bird in sight,

but before long dozens of seagulls would be circling overhead waiting for more, yelling and crying for handouts. Sometimes there would be fights on The Beach as a bigger gull would take a tasty chunk of fish away from a smaller tern. The sound of the gulls. That is definitely part of the Smith Beach Experience.

There are other sounds, too. We won't talk much about the obnoxious whine of the mosquito.

But, then, there was the sound of the distant horn buoys in the night. You certainly couldn't always hear them, but sometimes, if the night was still enough and the breeze was onshore to carry their sound, you could just hear their call way off across the water. And the sound of the wind in the trees. Especially on rainy days. And the evening calls of the bobwhites over in Tom Smith's fields on the other side of the road. Those are all part of the Smith Beach Experience.

Car horns, too. Whenever a friend would drive past, they'd honk their horn. We'd quickly crane our heads to see who it was. "There goes Charlie," or, "I guess Jimmy's headed up for the mail." It was all part of the Smith Beach Experience.

The sound of seagulls, and the sight of them swooping and soaring. The sea hawks, ospreys, too.

You'd see them hovering high in the sky, floating on the thermals. Then they would dive down into the pound nets to re-catch a fish before the fisherman whose pound nets they were could come out and empty them.

I remember once Retha was sitting on the top of her stairs when a big osprey flew over and dropped a huge speckled trout right in her lap! That was when Dad and Big Jim were going out to the approach to Hungars Creek and spending hours casting lures for specks early each morning, to no avail. And here Retha just sits on the top of her steps, and one gets delivered to her by airmail. Had a lot of good roe in it, too. Poor Dad, trying it the hard way.

Another distinctive sound at The Beach was Navy jets. We were right across the Bay from Norfolk Navy Base, and just northeast of Oceana Naval Air Station where the fighters from aircraft carriers would base when their carriers were in port. When the carriers were headed in, their fighters would take off while at sea and fly to Oceana, and then when the carrier returned to the sea, the fighters would fly back out and meet them. You would hear the noise first. A faint, but quickly increasing, screaming growl as the fighters, almost always flying in twos, got close. We'd excitedly (still do) look all around for them. But they were moving so fast, and were so low, that looking where the sound was coming from wouldn't work. They were way ahead of the noise. Then, all of a sudden, they would flash overhead, flying "close to the deck," and just as swiftly disappear. Way back when they used to regularly show off and rattle the windows by breaking the sound barrier, but I suppose there were too many complaints, and they don't do that anymore. Was exciting, though.

Television?

What did we do for excitement at Smith Beach? You pretty much had to make your own excitement. We never had television when we rented a cottage. There used to be a drive-in movie a ways up the road ... but it closed years ago.

No TV, so what did we do nights? Well, after a magnificent sunset we'd go out and walk.

Either on The Beach or on the road. Back then there were no streetlights on the road, and no "light pollution" to degrade the night's clarity. I've heard about the billions of stars that you can see when you are out in the middle of the ocean. Well, it can't be more than we'd see walking down The Beach. Awesome! The jet-black sky would be heavily powdered with stars. Mom would point out the different constellations for us. Dad would point out the different flashing lights on the black horizon. That flashing light over there was Wolf Trap Light. That one is Cabbage Patch. Sometimes we'd gather up driftwood, dig a hole, and have a bonfire on The Beach. The salt-impregnated wood would burn with beautiful colors.

Without electronic pastimes, though, windy days, when we couldn't go fishing, became more of a challenge. What to do? Well, believe it or not we would go sightseeing. Mom would find all sorts of places for us to go.

Would you believe an indoor rose farm? Several big hothouses packed with plant tables packed with rose bushes. Each bush was entered into the computer so that its output was carefully monitored, and when a given plant wasn't producing up to snuff it could be replaced. Water and nutrients were all carefully monitored and applied. A very scientific operation. Fascinating.

Another interesting place was the clam farm down on Cherrystone Creek. They grew their own "soup" to feed the little ones, move them from flat-to-flat as they grew, and would sell seed clams to commercial clamming operations. Pretty neat. Must work. There is now a clam farm down at The Gulf.

South of Cape Charles, off Route 13, is Custis Tomb. I used to get a real laugh out of this place. The story is that John Custis was a bachelor who finally married and brought his bride to his home, Arlington, on The Eastern Shore. It didn't take too long before he and his wife started arguing, and ultimately got to the point that they would only talk with each other through their house slave. One day he had the slave, Pompey, "Ask Mrs. Custis if she would like to go for a carriage ride." She responded in the affirmative, and he helped her up into the carriage and drove off ... albeit in chilly silence. They got down to the beach and were riding along the water's edge when Colonel Custis turned the carriage into The Bay. As the water came up to the floorboards, Mrs. Custis turned to her husband and asked, "Mr. Custis, where are you going?"

"To hell, madam, to hell."

"Drive on, Mr. Custis. Any place is better than Arlington with you."

"Madam, I believe you would as leave meet the Devil himself if I should drive to hell."

"Quite true, Sir," she answered. "I know you so well I would not be afraid to go anywhere you would go."

At that point Custis turned the carriage around and returned home. Upon his death Custis' direction had the following engraved on his tombstone:

> *Under this Marble Tomb lies ye Body of the Honorable John Custis Esqr. of the City of Williamsburg and Parish of Bruton Formerly of Hungars Parish and the Eastern Shore of Virginia and County of Northampton the Place of his Nativity Aged 71 years and Yet liv'd but Seven Years which was the space of time He kept a Batchelers house at Arlington on the Eastern Shore of Virginia.*

Always one for the last word, that John Custis.

We'd also go and visit homes and gardens. There are a lot of old colonial homes on The Shore, and many of them have formal gardens around them. We'd visit Pointe Farm on Savage Neck, and if we were lucky George Ames would be there and take us in for a tour. I remember he had a whiskey flask shaped like a big soft pretzel. Funny the things you remember. We also visited Eyre Hall, near Cheriton, and Vaucluse. In the gardens at Vaucluse was a sundial that was inscribed:

Time flies, you say?

Ah, no.

Time stays,

We *go!*

Fireworks

Fireworks! Now, that was some excitement at The Beach.

One-hour north of The Beach, just over the Maryland-Virginia border, is T-s Corner. It's at the Chincoteague turn-off. When driving down from our home in New Jersey we would usually stop there. Dad would buy some low-tax cigarettes, and we kids would stock up on Fireworks!!!!! For the mothers we'd also buy Roman candles and sparklers and pinwheels. The pretty stuff they could Oooh! and Aaaahhh! over. But us kids were interested in DESTRUCTION. FIRE-POWER. EXPLOSIONS. Yeah! Used to you could buy cherry bombs. And ashcans. And, later, M-80's! We'd usually have to do it on the sly, moms not being excited about the prospect of blown-off fingers and such. But when we got our armaments down to the beach, look out! Anything was fair game, and we tried to be creative in our destruction.

Walking down the beach at low tide, one time, we found a square five-gallon gas can. Guess it washed up with the tide. It was empty, so we put it out on an exposed sandbar, dropped in a cherry bomb, and ran. The can must have still had some sort of flammable residue in it 'cause when the explosion split it open the flames were brief but spectacular!

Another time we found an old commode, sitting upright and full of sand. You never knew what would show up on the beach. We scooped out the sand in the bowl on one side, put a board with sand on top of it partially covering the hole, building a bunker, and dropped in a cherry bomb. Porcelain really doesn't have much structural integrity.

Then, at night we would put on our own Fourth of July spectaculars, with the mothers ooohing and aaaahhing up on the bank. Oh, and constantly warning us to be careful and not burn ourselves, of course. Yeah, that was another part of the Smith Beach Experience. Then they stopped selling the exploding fireworks at T's Corner. Of course, if you knew John Bruce White you could occasionally buy some ashcans under-the-counter at his store, close to Cheriton, but his store's been gone for years, now.

Just up the beach from us someone built a wooden platform in the shallows, about twenty feet off the beach. Turns out it was for some really serious Fourth of July fireworks. How cool! A not-quite professional extravaganza right there where we wouldn't have to travel to be entertained. Of course, that was many years ago. Doesn't happen anymore.

Excitement?

What do we do for excitement at Smith Beach? Well, one year someone put up a dancehall down at the end of the road, at The Gulf. I guess that was exciting, for some. I know the parents were not real happy about it. However, it didn't last long as a dancehall. Closed after about a year. It's been someone's residence for years, now. And up at the head of the road, by B&B (well, Eastville Supermarket), there used to be a soft ice cream stand. Right across the street. How cosmopolitan! It didn't last long. After about a year it became a residence. Then it became a little church. Last I looked it was back to being a home.

And just south of that Kate opened her Kupboard. A bakery. There is nothing like a warm cinnamon sticky bun fresh out of the oven! Get up early in the morning, put the coffee on, and drive up to Kate's to buy sticky buns for breakfast! Mmmmmm! Kate opened one of her Kupboards up the road in Exmore, too. Then when the Exmore Kupboard was doing well, Kate closed the one in Eastville. That was years ago.

Then on the other side of the ice cream stand/home/church/home was a hardware store. Nice big steel structure. Fishing supplies, tools, etc. When we showed up the next year it was used cars. It's a residence, now.

Up in Eastville is the two-story Eastville Inn. Can't have a county seat without an Inn. I remember that's where I first ate a Slim Jim®. The Inn had a wooden screen door with a spring on it that slammed the door when it closed. Remember those? I don't remember if they ever let rooms for as long as I've known it. There was a restaurant in the Inn, but that closed years ago. Someone has been restoring the Inn, but that's been going on for years, now, and it's not open yet.

Across the street from the Eastville Inn was a drugstore. That was convenient, too, and lasted for a while. When it closed it was re-opened as an antique shop. I don't know how well they did as an antique shop, but it closed years ago.

And across the street from the courthouse was Shrieve's Texaco. If you were ordering something from Sears that had to be delivered UPS, you had it delivered to the Texaco station. They'd hold it for you, and if you had one of the few telephones at the Beach, they would call and let you know it was there. The Texaco station has been gone, now, for decades.

Story Telling

With no television, visiting and story-telling were popular evening pastimes. Charlie always told such great stories about when he was a kid on The Shore. He told, once, about the time his brother was teaching him how to chop the head off a chicken to get it ready for dinner. Hold the wing tips and legs with one hand, put her across the block, and CHOP! Off with her head! Charlie grabbed the hen, put her across the block, swung his hatchet ... and flinched! Cut off the tip of her beak. The hen wrenched loose and started racing around the yard with Charlie racing after her. She was too fast, and Charlie said, "I had to go get my gun and shoot her or we wouldn't have eaten." Then he'd rear back and laugh and laugh.

One time, when we were walking around on a little deserted island out in The Bay, Charlie gave me a little sprig of something and told me to put it in my shoe for good luck. He said that he had, as a kid, and the next day the schoolhouse burned down.

Charlie was always good at pulling our legs. Dad put one over on Charlie one day, though. Charlie was making a communion table for his church and was real proud of it. Charlie was quite a craftsman. He had hand-carved the table's front rail. It was a beautiful job. When Charlie took Dad to look at the table, Dad turned to Charlie and asked, Charlie, how do you spell "REMEMBRANCE?" Charlie had carved IN REMEMBRANCE OF ME on the front rail of the communion table. Charlie started looking. The longer he looked, the more unsure of the spelling he became, until he was really flummoxed. He hadn't spelled it wrong, of course. Dad never said that he had. He only asked what the proper spelling was, and, of course, once the doubt was planted it only got worse and worse. It was probably the best one Dad ever put over on Charlie. But I digress.

Fishing

What is there exciting to do at Smith Beach? Well, with all the water out there, one thing is definitely fishing. Fishing. You ever see the bumper sticker that says, A BAD DAY FISHING IS BETTER THAN A GOOD DAY AT THE OFFICE? That was really our main pastime. When we started going to The Beach we would stop in Maryland to rent a 5 hp outboard motor. When we got to The Beach Big Jim would call his friend who was a waterman up Hungars Creek, and he would let us borrow one of his workboats for the two weeks we would be there. We would all drive over to his place, and he would tow a big 20' scow over to where we were at the Beach.

Now, for those of you who don't know, a scow is a big, wooden, flat-bottomed work boat, and that's all this was. No frills. Heck, not even any seats. We would walk up and down the beach until we had scavenged up a few planks we could put across the gunnels for the adults to sit on. Us kids would sit on up-turned peach or bushel baskets. We'd hang that little 5 hp on the back, and away we would go. Four adults and four kids in a boat that weighed a ton. But we were fishing! The scow we borrowed would usually have a hole drilled in the bottom with a wooden plug in it. This was so the waterman could let in some water to wash the mud or whatever off the bottom. Then there would generally be an old coal shovel which would be used to bail the grubby water back out. I remember at least once when Big Jim was moving around the boat, not paying attention to his feet, that he kicked the plug out, and water started flooding into the boat, which was weighted down with eight fishermen. Then there'd be a frantic search for the plug, screams from the kids, panic, and then the work of bailing once things came under control.

There are lots of fishing holes, out in front of The Beach. Back before many folks had Loran or GPS or depth finders on their small boats, we used to drift around until we seemed to find a hole where the fish were biting, and then we'd use triangulation to set the location. You see, that duck blind is right on that point of land up by Honeymoon Island, and over there that dead tree is right on the corner of the deserted hotel. That's how we'd know we were on Big Rock. Or was it Little Rock? The one was farther out into the Bay. Whatever. It worked real well, until someone cut down the tree by the deserted hotel as a prank. I know who did it, but I'll never tell. Back then, when they did it, folks were kind of upset. They had to find their fishing holes all over again, and re-triangulate. One year Willard put some orange-painted Clorox containers out to mark one of the Rocks, but they've been gone for years, now. So's Willard, for that matter.

Once we'd got our courage up we'd go way out, to The Cell. The Cell was an old Navy degaussing station from WWII. From the beach it looked kind of like an old steam locomotive and coal car sitting out in the middle of The Bay. I guess there was lots of stuff growing from the parts of The Cell that were under the water, 'cause the fish used to like to gather round it and eat. Each year, after the winter storms, it seemed like another part of The Cell was missing when we'd show up for vacation. One year the smokestack was gone, and the next another big chunk was missing. Seemed to take a long time for all of it to disappear, but The Cell's been gone for years, now. Dad used to recall how he took the ship he skippered through The Cell, back in the War. That was before all it was good for was fishing. It is still a popular place, and on nice fishing days from shore you can see the tiny white specks and the flash of sun on windshields of the boats out there.

Mostly, back in the early days, we used clams or peeler crabs for bait. A peeler was a hard-shell crab that was just about to molt, and when you peeled off the hard shell there was the newly formed soft shell just beneath. On days where the fishing was particularly good we would keep some of the hard-shell crabs that would grab our bait on the bottom and hang on for the ride to the surface. That happened a lot, and sometimes we would go home with almost as many hard-shell blue crabs as fish. I remember one year when we came in from fishing and left a basket with some hard crabs in it outside while we cleaned up and ate dinner. There was a stray cat around, and it kept sniffing at those strange smells coming from the basket with the crabs. Suddenly we heard a rowwwwrrrrrrrr that raised the hair on the back of our necks as the cat found out what the crabs had for defense. The crab must have grabbed hold and hung on for the ride because we could hear the cat race around the outside of the cottage, then slam into one corner, apparently knocking the crab off. Curiosity didn't kill it, but it sure gave it a bloody nose!

Since we are talking about fishing and crabs this might be a good place to mention crabbing. Fifty years ago, the Chesapeake Bay was, while perhaps not pristine, reasonably clean. One marker of this were the fields of grass growing in the shallows. We kids hated the grass because we were always afraid that there were crabs hiding in there that would pinch our toes. And there were!

Blue crabs were plentiful enough, back then, that we would put a bushel basket in an inflated innertube, tie it to our waists with a ten-foot length of line, and go crabbing with a dip net. That was really fun. You would slowly walk through the shallow water watching for crabs, and when you found one you would try to quickly scoop him up and dump him into the basket. Honestly, we could half fill a bushel basket dipping crabs.

Out in front of the house, in the channel, were usually a line of crab pots. Traps. You'd know them from the distinctive colored floats used to mark each one of them. Each crabber would paint his floats differently so you would know to whom each line of pots belonged. You would see them, generally twice a day, slowly working their line of pots, pulling them, emptying the crabs into their boat, re-baiting the trap and then tossing them back, all without stopping.

These traps represented a waterman's livelihood, and it was illegal to mess with them, much less pull them and help yourself to the contents. As kids we would occasionally pull a trap just to see what was in there, but mostly we just used the floats to waterski around.

On occasion we would go to a waterman's to buy peelers for bait. One of these was "Little Haynie." He had a facility — no, that's too grandiose — he had a shack on, I think, Cherrystone Creek. His working shack was on pilings over the water, and all around were floats — shallow, wooden slat, floating pens — in which he kept his crabs. Most of Haynie's business was shipping softshell crabs to restaurants up north. In the floats were the crabs, and he and his men would watch them until they were ready to molt. You could tell how close they were by looking through their flipper to see the new shell forming.

Once their new shell was ready, and they started their molt, they became "busters." They were busting out of their hard shells. At this point it was essential to get them out of the flats where the other crabs were, or they would be eaten by the crabs who were still hard. They didn't use a net, as that would be time consuming when the crabs got tangled. They used what almost looked like a squash racquet — flat, round, with a tight netting in the middle. Like a spatula they'd use this to flip the buster into a container where he'd be closely watched until he exited his hard shell. Then he'd be scooped up and put on a layer of seaweed and ice in a crate for shipping.

Hefty used to "farm" soft-shells at the Beach. He'd put a bunch of drain tiles out in the shallows, up and down the Beach, and then check them every day to see if they were being used. Crabs getting ready to bust would go into these tiles to hide from predators until they had their new shells hard, when they would be able to protect themselves. Couldn't hide from Hefty, though.

In those days the other primary fishing bait we used was clam. Mostly when using them for bait we'd buy them. But if we wanted them to eat, then it was time to go clamming.

We would wait until the tide was low, then all climb into the boat (we did not think of it as a scow) and head to the sandbars just out of the mouth of the Gulf. While the kids played in the shallow water the fathers would take long-tined clam rakes and walk long furrows, generally through the grass. They'd pull the rakes through until they heard a scraping sound, dig down under it, and (hopefully) pull up a clam, which they'd toss into that same bushel-basket-in-innertube floating behind them.

Sometimes they would think they found a big clam, but what they'd pull up would be what we called a "conch," but which I think is actually a whelk.

If it didn't have anyone living in it, we'd take it along as a souvenir. Use it to mark out the edge of the front garden.

Meanwhile the mothers were walking in waist-deep water, kind of scrooching down with their toes. Mom was really good at finding clams this way, and lots of times we kids would then dive down and dig the clam out from under mom's feet.

Clamming was usually pretty good, if a lot of work. Uncle Carl Weisiger sure enjoyed it. He'd pull up a clam that was kind of small, throw it with force into the basket, then say, "Aw, that one broke. Guess I'll have to eat it now." Wash it off in the salty Bay water and slurp it down. You don't get seafood fresher than that.

When we'd get back with all our clams we'd stick a pole upright in the shallow water out in front of the house, for a marker, and plant the clams around the pole to keep them available until we wanted to eat them. Sometimes instead of the pole we'd take an old tire, put it out in the shallows, and put the clams in the sand in the middle of the tire.

Then there was the day that a neighbor, someone who was not a "regular" at Smith Beach, told us that we were wasting our time going all the way to The Gulf for our clams. Why, he had been clamming right off the beach, and found a whole bed of clams! Dug up almost a bushel full! You guessed it. He had found our stock of planted clams. I don't know if Dad and Poppa Jim ever did tell him what he had done. After all, he just didn't know any better. Didn't bother me any. I wasn't going to eat any of those nasty things (ah, the ignorance of youth)!

Clamming has kind of gone south with the crabbing and the quality of the water.

Stuff Washed Up

Whereas here in Florida beach combing usually means either sea shelling or roaming around with a metal detector, beach combing at the Beach is more eclectic. You never know just what you will find.

One year Little Jim and I found a little wooden punt. The name painted on the transom was "Flea." The Flea was busted up and waterlogged, and we were pretty certain no one at the Beach was looking for it. But we had a ball with it, once we got it dried out and sort-of caulked some of the seams. We never actually took it anywhere, but when you are an 8 or 10-year-old kid, a hulk like this becomes a veritable pirate frigate.

Another time it was a pretty nice fiberglass boat that had washed up and had the bad luck of coming to rest against some riprap someone had dumped to try to protect their bank. It was busted all to pieces. Nothing even for a kid to salvage.

The ferry, that we mentioned before, was replaced in in 1964 by the Chesapeake Bay Bridge Tunnel. On the Eastern Shore end of the CBBT is a "high bridge", designed to allow good-sized fishing boats to pass underneath. One day an elderly couple stopped on the down-side of the bridge to take pictures. Unfortunately, at that time the roadway was only two-lane, and a tractor trailer headed north from Florida topped the rise and couldn't stop before plowing into the stopped car. The trailer went over the side, and mom and dad picked up enough grapefruit from the beach over the next couple of weeks to keep them until the winter.

The Norfolk-Newport News area used to be a big terminus for shipping coal overseas. One year there was a strike in the coal mines, and there was nothing to ship for some months. I remember driving over the CBBT and seeing dozens of colliers anchored off Virginia Beach waiting for some coal to haul. Later that summer dad told me that they were picking up the most interesting trash on the beach, stuff that had been tossed overboard from the foreign colliers. You just never know.

Sometimes what washes up is not as interesting. The other day it was hundreds of good-sized dead fish washed up on the sand. Three bunker boats purse seining for menhaden had been working just off the beach for most of the week. These dead fish are what they call the "by catch," the additional fish that are scooped in the nets and later discarded because they aren't the right ones. And they wonder why fishing has gotten so bad.

Some are appreciative, though. I watched as two ghost crabs delicately feasted on two of the carcasses. I've located one of their burrows, too. I'd love to try to get some photos of them, but they are very skittish. I swear, I'm thirty yards away from them, and elevated fifteen feet, and I still think they "feel" me watching them.

I don't know what the system is, but the crab eats for a while, and then walks back up the beach from the water's edge. They are land crabs, so their legs are designed for walking, not swimming, and when they walk they mince delicately on their tiptoes like hard-shelled ballerinas. When the two crabs pass each other, they glare fiercely as the sidle sideways past, holding their pinchers up threateningly. And that's interesting. A blue crab will hold his pinchers up more-or-less horizontally to ward off attackers. These guys' pinchers kind of hang down, when they lift them up, in an almost karate-looking pose.

Well, That's It

Well, that's it. That is my sketchbook of memories from over 60 years' vacationing on The Eastern Shore. I am certain there is much I have forgotten.

So much has changed at Smith Beach, over the years. And yet everything remains the same. That's the beauty of The Eastern Shore, at least the Lower Shore, and Smith Beach. It is a way of life that has been proven by time and tradition. It shows that you can be surrounded by the manic bustle of modern life, but still remain gentle and genteel. It shows that there can be things more important than a dollar – like history and tradition and manners and civility and friends and a tried and true way of country life. Those of us who look to the Lower Shore and Smith Beach as an anchor or normalcy in our frantic rat race lives can only pray that the forces of development (development does not necessarily equal progress) and the quest for the almighty dollar do not ultimately destroy what for now is such a joy.

PHILOSOPHICAL REFLECTIONS ON SHOREBIRDS

Have you ever considered a comparative study of bird flight? No, really! Sitting here, at the Beach, I've had an opportunity to indulge myself in some deep philosophical reflections, one of which has been the flight characteristics of birds relative to species and assumed psycho/social proclivities. I find that it is a very underrated yet intellectually stimulating field of study.

Contemplate the following: Seagulls tend to be scavengers. Whenever possible they do not do their own foraging for food ... they eat whatever garbage they can find wherever they happen to find it. Of course, they are pretty egalitarian about it. Once they find a source for a free meal they call all their buddies to join in. [They are a lot like charities in that way. Once you give to one, hundreds seem to come out of the woodwork looking for handouts.] But essentially Seagulls are lazy. They are very laid back, and their flight patterns reflect it. They fly with a very economical wing movement. A little up, a little down, and if there is a wind, coast as much as possible. They always seem to be going somewhere, but there is little agreement on where that is. Some are heading this way while others are heading that. No seeming rhyme or reason.

The Brown Pelicans, on the other hand, all seem to know just where they are headed. There is usually a string of five--or-so of them, gracefully skimming just at wavetop height. Very self-assured. It seems you seldom see them move their wings at all ... almost as though they have a built-in tailwind keeping them aloft. Stately. They don't really care what other fowl are up to. Indeed, it seems beneath them to even consider the question. Of course, their veneer of elegance is rudely ripped away when they come in for a landing. Then their aerodynamic properties change from glider to bowling ball as they crash into the water with all the grace and beauty of a pregnant warthog. Pseudo-sophisticates.

Pigeons are the real obsessive-compulsives. They fly so hard that you can hear their wings slapping together! It's almost as though they have a built-in head wind that they constantly must fight. And they simply cannot fly off on their own. Paranoiacally they are always afraid that some other Pigeon is going to get something they aren't. That's why you always see them flying in large flocks, and always changing directions. "Hey, where's that guy going?" And they all swoop off in that direction. "Wait a minute ... look where he is headed!" And they all fly off after him. Neurotics! Every one of them.

Sandpipers don't fly too much. They are the maiden aunts of the bird world. Sandpipers bustle around the sand, sticking their nose [well, bill] in here, and then in there, and then following the water as it goes out, AND THEN RUNNING LIKE CRAZY AS IT COMES BACK IN. [You'd think they'd learn the trick, but they keep wandering out as the waves retreat, AND THEN FRANTICALLY RUNNING TO KEEP THEIR FEET DRY. Not smart.]

Then there is the solitary Osprey. Don't even think about messing with him. He slowly, regally, beats the air with his wings, soaring up in the sky, until ... suddenly ... **HEFOLDSHISWINGSANDDIVESINTOTHEWATERB EFOREYOUCANBLINK!** Then he shakes off the water and the bonds of the earth and fights his way skyward with slow, powerful strokes as he carries his catch back to the nest. Self-sufficient. Autonomous. Stately. Imperious. Introverted overachievers?

I guess the Canada Geese are the Jewish mothers. The yentas. They all cluster around in one big crowd, and then they take off en masse, with such a honking and talking and carrying on ... sounds like a Hadassah meeting when the refreshments have run out. Everyone talking, no one listening, oy!

There is a bird over here called the Black Skimmer. I guess he is the teenager of the crowd. He has a terrible underbite (the only bird whose lower mandible is longer than his upper), which might be the reason for his show-offy behavior. He spends his day, usually with a date, flying at breakneck speed, skimming through the shallows with his bottom lip [well, bill] dragging in the water. Kind of like a perpetual pout. I KNOW his mother must have told him, "If you keep doing that your face will freeze like that." Just another adenoidal mouth-breather trying to be cool. I can't help but wonder what would happen if that lower lip hooked a good-sized fish.

Another teenager hoist on his own petard.

I remember watching the Swallows that nested under the wharf up in Maine. They were like hyperactive children who had forgotten to take their Ritalin®. Good grief! Swooping and darting and diving, here and there and back again! You just know that somewhere there is a mother Swallow, feathers gray and ragged, looking for a government program to narcotize her frenetic children before she flips out completely ... Ritalin® for them, Prozac® for her.

Then, of course, there is the neighborhood intimidator. Come on, you know who I mean. That's right, the Mockingbird. Sits up on the peak of the roof, chest puffed out, telling everyone about how cool he is. Then when the poor dog wanders out to take a leak, old Mockingbird pops up, locks his wings in attack mode, and dive-bombs the heck out of her. Pecks her head and her rear, when all she is doing is looking for the proper place to poop. He thinks he's so cool. He better remember that "It's a sin to kill a mockingbird" will only take you so far. Bully.

You see? Calm reflections by the soothing water of The Chesapeake Bay can lead to truly seminal philosophical discoveries on the nature of life and living things. Or do you think I've been out of touch for a touch too long?

Other Books by David Thatcher Wilson

The Demon Series is a series of books about Ezkeel, a minor demon who tries to spread evil, but gets thwarted each time, as he travels from Haiti to Hialeah and other cities. He tries, has some successes, but ultimately is exorcised, or at least kicked out.

Quite apart from the Ezkeel books is MUSINGS. MUSINGS helps you see beyond the commonplace and more fully appreciate and enjoy all that surrounds you. It is not preachy. It is not sectarian. It is just one person's MUSINGS about the things he sees every day. Why should you read it? Hopefully it will enable you to actually see, rather than just look.

Also, if you would be so kind, please go to Amazon and review AN EASTERN SHORE SKETCHBOOK. I really do want to know what you think of it.

God bless!

David Thatcher Wilson
Ft. Lauderdale, Florida
September 17, 2016

david@davidthatcherwilson.com
www.davidthatcherwilson.com
www.facebook.com/davidthatcherwilson